YOU CAN DRAW IT!

HORSES

WRITTEN BY JON EPPARD
ILLUSTRATED BY STEVE PORTER

BELLWETHER MEDIA · MINNEAPOLIS, MN

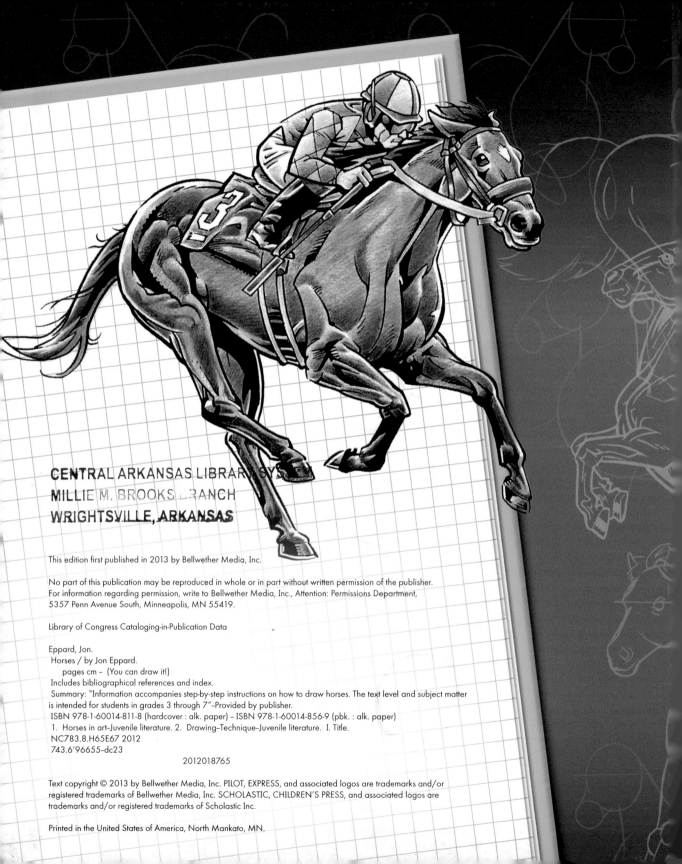

This edition first published in 2013 by Bellwether Media, Inc.

No part of this publication may be reproduced in whole or in part without written permission of the publisher.
For information regarding permission, write to Bellwether Media, Inc., Attention: Permissions Department,
5357 Penn Avenue South, Minneapolis, MN 55419.

Library of Congress Cataloging-in-Publication Data

Eppard, Jon.
 Horses / by Jon Eppard.
      pages cm – (You can draw it!)
 Includes bibliographical references and index.
  Summary: "Information accompanies step-by-step instructions on how to draw horses. The text level and subject matter
is intended for students in grades 3 through 7"–Provided by publisher.
  ISBN 978-1-60014-811-8 (hardcover : alk. paper) – ISBN 978-1-60014-856-9 (pbk. : alk. paper)
  1. Horses in art–Juvenile literature. 2. Drawing–Technique–Juvenile literature. I. Title.
 NC783.8.H65E67 2012
 743.6'96655–dc23

                                2012018765

Printed in the United States of America, North Mankato, MN.

TABLE OF CONTENTS

HORSES!

For thousands of years, horses have helped humans in many ways. Large horses have helped farmers plow fields and pull heavy loads. Fast horses have carried riders and messages over long distances. Brave horses have charged into famous battles. Today, the variety of horse breeds allows people to use them for specific purposes. Owners form strong bonds with their horses and often think of them as part of the family.

DRAWING FROM PHOTOS IS A GREAT PLACE TO START. WORK YOUR WAY UP TO DRAWING FROM MEMORY OR YOUR IMAGINATION.

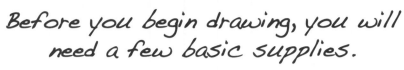

Before you begin drawing, you will need a few basic supplies.

PAPER

DRAWING PENCILS

BLACK INK PEN

2B OR NOT 2B?

NOT ALL DRAWING PENCILS ARE THE SAME. "B" PENCILS ARE SOFTER, MAKE DARKER MARKS, AND SMUDGE EASILY. "H" PENCILS ARE HARDER, MAKE LIGHTER MARKS, AND DON'T SMUDGE VERY MUCH AT ALL.

COLORED PENCILS
(ALL DRAWINGS IN THIS BOOK WERE FINISHED WITH COLORED PENCILS.)

ERASER

PENCIL SHARPENER

Arabian Horse
The Wind Rider

Known for their beauty and speed, Arabian horses are one of the most popular breeds in the world. Their intelligence, **endurance**, and **temperament** make them desirable for **dressage** and long-distance competitions. Arabians have earned their nickname, "Drinkers of the Wind."

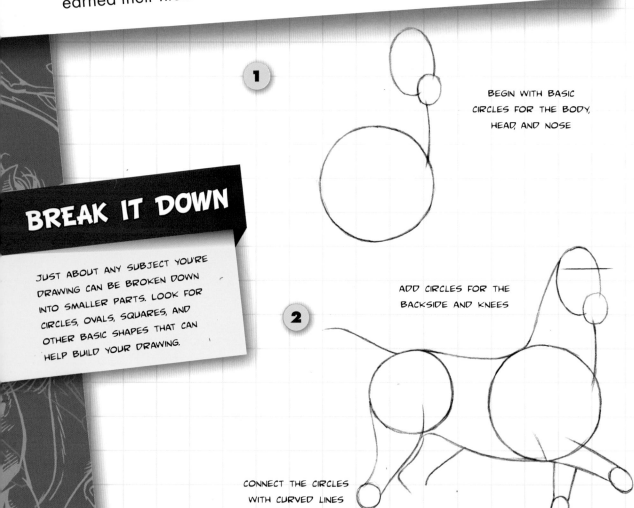

1 BEGIN WITH BASIC CIRCLES FOR THE BODY, HEAD, AND NOSE

2 ADD CIRCLES FOR THE BACKSIDE AND KNEES

CONNECT THE CIRCLES WITH CURVED LINES

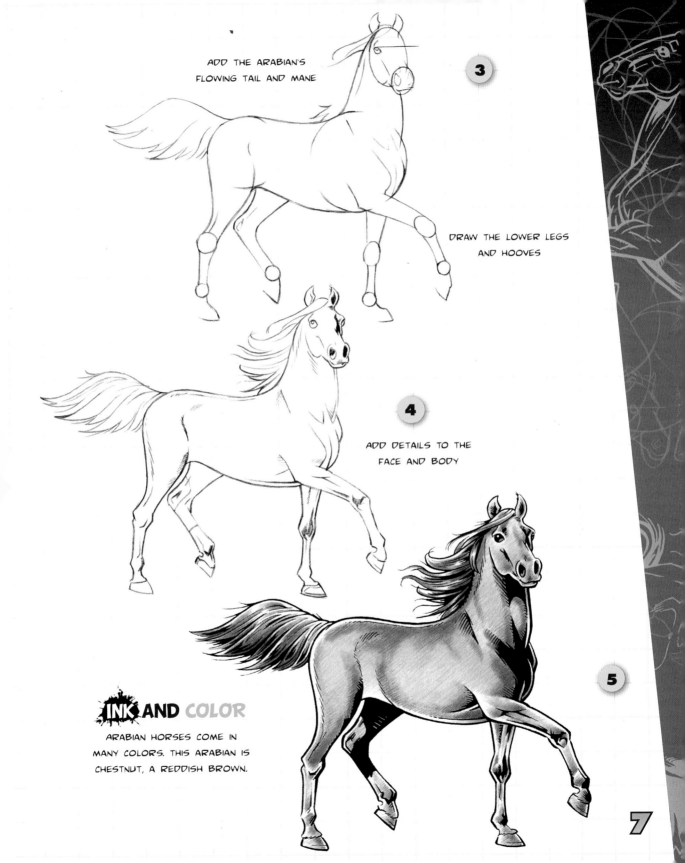

ADD THE ARABIAN'S
FLOWING TAIL AND MANE

3

DRAW THE LOWER LEGS
AND HOOVES

4

ADD DETAILS TO THE
FACE AND BODY

5

INK AND COLOR

ARABIAN HORSES COME IN
MANY COLORS. THIS ARABIAN IS
CHESTNUT, A REDDISH BROWN.

7

Clydesdale Horse
The Gentle Giant

Clippety-clop, clippety-clop. This is the sound of Clydesdales parading through crowded city streets. The rhythm of their hooves is as steady as their nature. Throughout history, Clydesdales have used their size and strength for many jobs. In the **Middle Ages**, they carried knights into battle. Centuries later, farmers turned them into **driving horses**. Today these gentle giants entertain at competitions and parades, where they dwarf all who stand beside them!

KEEP YOUR EDGE!

TO AVOID SHARPENING TOO MUCH, ROTATE YOUR PENCIL SLIGHTLY TO FIND A SHARP EDGE.

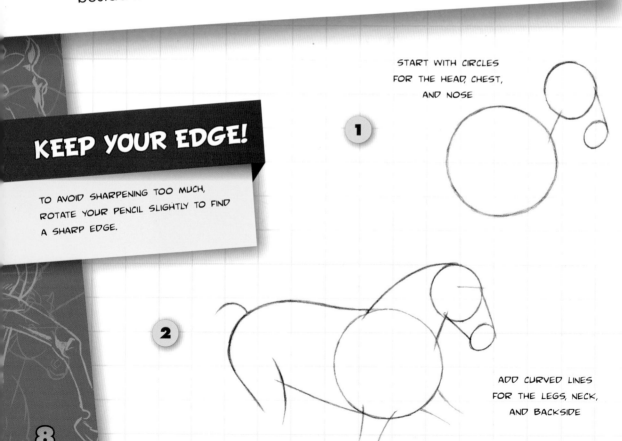

1 START WITH CIRCLES FOR THE HEAD, CHEST, AND NOSE

2 ADD CURVED LINES FOR THE LEGS, NECK, AND BACKSIDE

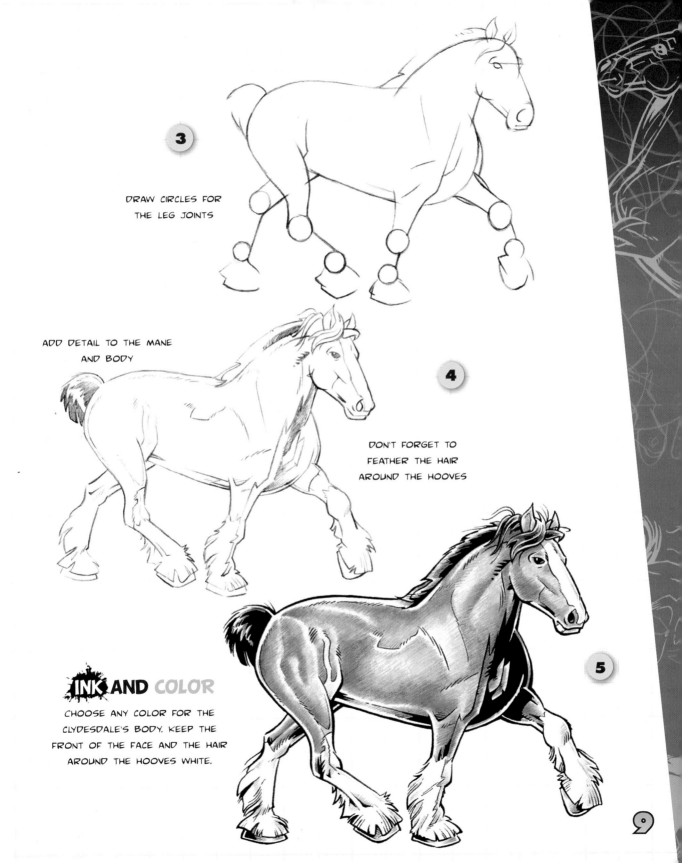

3

DRAW CIRCLES FOR
THE LEG JOINTS

ADD DETAIL TO THE MANE
AND BODY

4

DON'T FORGET TO
FEATHER THE HAIR
AROUND THE HOOVES

INK AND COLOR

CHOOSE ANY COLOR FOR THE
CLYDESDALE'S BODY. KEEP THE
FRONT OF THE FACE AND THE HAIR
AROUND THE HOOVES WHITE.

5

Morgan Horse
The First American Breed

In the late 1700s, Justin Morgan had a horse named Figure. Figure had exceptional strength for his small, slender body. Other people wanted horses like Figure. He soon became the **foundation horse** of a brand-new breed. Today Morgan horses compete in many events and continue to work on farms throughout the United States.

STAY BACK

HOLD YOUR PENCIL A LITTLE FARTHER BACK FROM THE TIP. THIS ALLOWS YOU TO DRAW LONGER, SMOOTHER LINES.

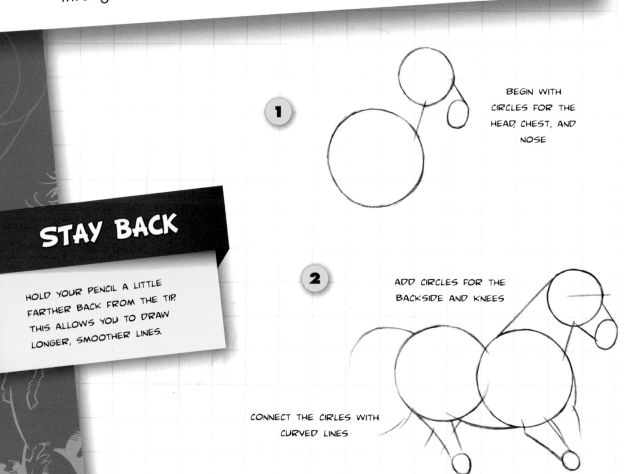

1 BEGIN WITH CIRCLES FOR THE HEAD, CHEST, AND NOSE

2 ADD CIRCLES FOR THE BACKSIDE AND KNEES

CONNECT THE CIRLES WITH CURVED LINES

LIGHTLY DRAW LINES FOR
THE TAIL AND MANE

3

DON'T FORGET
TO ADD
THE HOOVES

DRAW THE DETAILS FOR
THE EYES AND MANE

4

ADD SHADING
DETAILS

INK AND COLOR

MAKE THIS HORSE A BLACK BEAUTY.
ACCENT ITS DARK COAT WITH
BROWNS AND BLUES.

5

Paint Horse
The Showstopper

Paint horses are multicolored marvels that often star in the show ring. They are all-around rodeo horses and champion barrel racers. In barrel racing, horses weave around three barrels under the guidance of their riders. It's no surprise when the quick and intelligent Paint horse completes the course in record time!

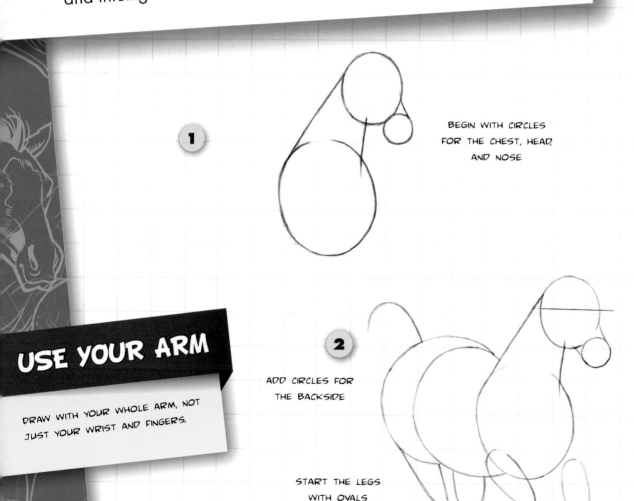

1 BEGIN WITH CIRCLES FOR THE CHEST, HEAD, AND NOSE

USE YOUR ARM

DRAW WITH YOUR WHOLE ARM, NOT JUST YOUR WRIST AND FINGERS.

2 ADD CIRCLES FOR THE BACKSIDE

START THE LEGS WITH OVALS

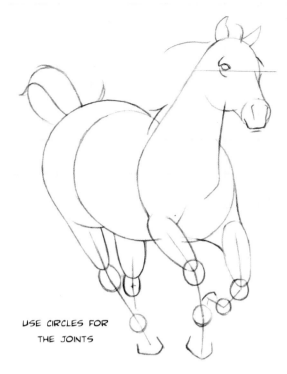

3

OUTLINE THE TAIL, EYES, EARS, AND NOSE

ADD DETAIL TO THE TAIL, FACE, AND BODY

USE CIRCLES FOR THE JOINTS

4

5

INK AND COLOR

RESEARCH PAINT HORSE COAT COLORS AND CHOOSE YOUR FAVORITE. MAKE SURE TO KEEP SECTIONS OF THE HORSE WHITE.

Lipizzan Horse
The Ballet Dancer

Lipizzans are known as "the dancing white stallions" because they are masters of classical dressage. They march, leap, and kick in harmony with classical music as their riders direct them. The most talented Lipizzans can perform a series of complex movements called the **Airs Above the Ground**. These movements were once used to intimidate the enemy in ancient battles.

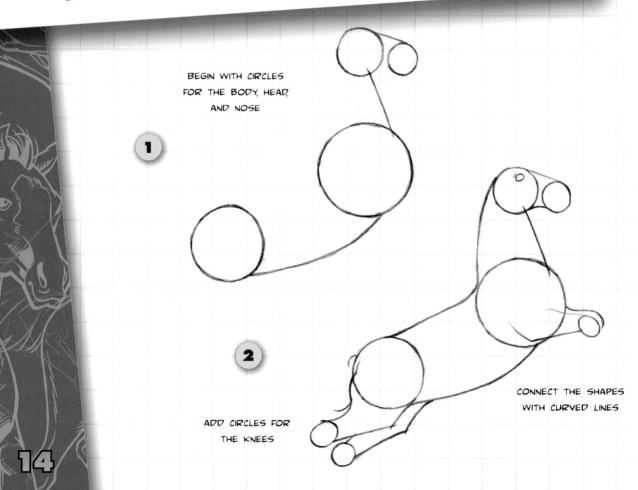

BEGIN WITH CIRCLES FOR THE BODY, HEAD, AND NOSE

1

2

ADD CIRCLES FOR THE KNEES

CONNECT THE SHAPES WITH CURVED LINES

LIGHTLY ADD LINES FOR
THE MANE AND TAIL

DRAW THE DETAILS FOR
THE EYES AND NOSE

3

ADD TO
THE LEGS

LIGHT TO DARK

BEGIN YOUR DRAWING WITH VERY
LIGHT LINES. SLOWLY BUILD UP TO
DARK LINES AS YOU REACH THE
FINAL STEPS. THIS WILL ALLOW FOR
EASY CORRECTION OF MISTAKES.

ADD SHADING DETAILS

4

5

INK AND COLOR

LIPIZZANS CAN BE A VERY LIGHT
BLUEISH GRAY OR COMPLETELY
WHITE. ACCENT THIS LIPIZZAN WITH
GRAYS AND BLUES.

Shetland Pony
The Little Spitfire

The small, sassy Shetland pony came from the Shetland Islands off the northeast coast of Scotland. Throughout history, Shetlands have been used to transport goods, work on farms, and even haul coal in mines. Don't let their size fool you! Shetlands are hard workers, and today they can be found competing in **harness racing** and **pole bending** events around the world.

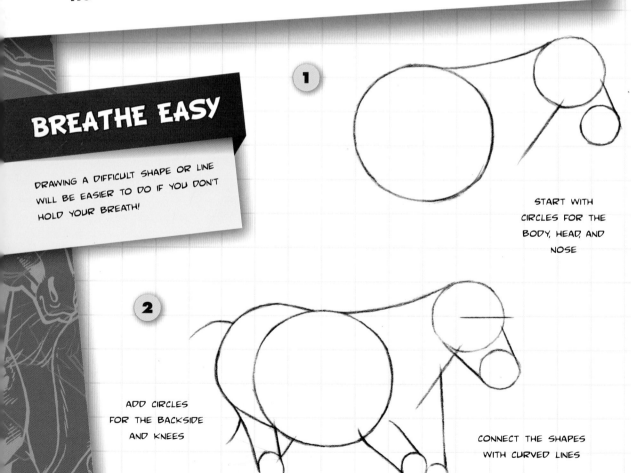

1

START WITH CIRCLES FOR THE BODY, HEAD, AND NOSE

2

ADD CIRCLES FOR THE BACKSIDE AND KNEES

CONNECT THE SHAPES WITH CURVED LINES

LIGHTLY ADD LINES
FOR THE MANE
AND TAIL

3

DRAW THE HOOVES

4

DRAW DETAILS FOR THE
MANE, TAIL, AND FACE

5

INK AND COLOR

USE CONTRAST ON THIS SHETLAND.
COLOR THE BODY DARK AND MAKE
THE MANE AND TAIL CREAMY WHITE.

17

Appaloosa Horse
The Native American Breed

Spotted horses have a long history. Originating in Europe and Asia, they made their way to the Americas in the 1500s. A Native American tribe called the Nez Perce **crossbred** their best horses. The result was the Appaloosa. Today, the intelligent breed is a favorite in jumping competitions and pole bending.

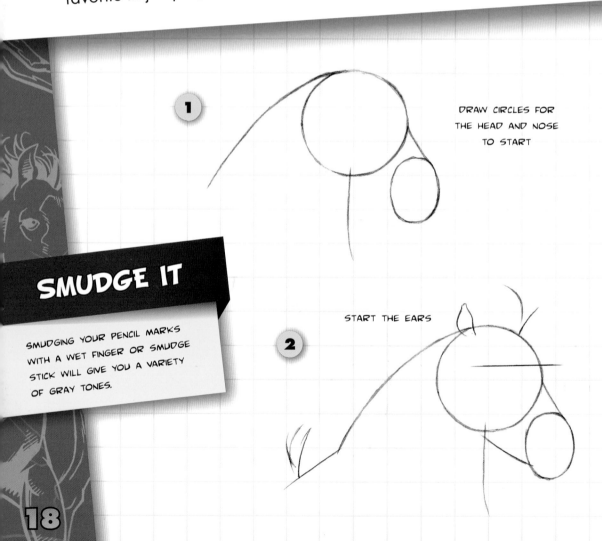

1 DRAW CIRCLES FOR THE HEAD AND NOSE TO START

2 START THE EARS

SMUDGE IT

SMUDGING YOUR PENCIL MARKS WITH A WET FINGER OR SMUDGE STICK WILL GIVE YOU A VARIETY OF GRAY TONES.

ADD THE NOSE
AND EYES

3

LIGHTLY DRAW THE
FLOWING MANE

DON'T FORGET THE
APPALOOSA'S SPOTS

4

INK AND COLOR

APPALOOSAS CAN HAVE
DIFFERENT COAT COLORS AND
PATTERNS. USE BLACK AND
WHITE TO SHOW CONTRAST.

5

19

Thoroughbred Horse
The Track Star

Racing is in the Thoroughbred's blood. This horse is built for speed and destined for the track. At just 18 months old, young Thoroughbreds begin working with **jockeys**. The fastest ones compete for the **Triple Crown** at the age of three. A racehorse must make it to the winner's circle three times in the same year to earn this title!

MIX AND MATCH

YOU CAN MIX COLORS BY GOING OVER A PREVIOUSLY COLORED SECTION WITH A NEW COLOR.

1

BEGIN THE JOCKEY WITH AN OVAL AND CIRCLE

START THE HORSE WITH CIRCLES FOR THE CHEST, HEAD, AND NOSE

ADD LINES FOR THE HORSE'S LEGS AND THE JOCKEY'S ARMS

2

DRAW CIRCLES FOR THE BACKSIDE AND KNEES OF THE HORSE

ADD LINES FOR THE SADDLE
AND REINS

3

ADD THE DETAILS
ON THE JOCKEY

COMPLETE THE LEGS
AND HOOVES

4

SHADE PARTS OF
THE MANE, NOSE,
AND LEGS

5

INK AND COLOR

THOROUGHBREDS CAN BE MANY
COLORS. THIS HORSE IS DARK
BROWN WITH A BLACK TAIL AND
MANE. CHOOSE BRIGHT COLORS FOR
THE JOCKEY'S UNIFORM.

21

GLOSSARY

Airs Above the Ground—a style of classical dressage in which horses lift their front hooves or their bodies off the ground

crossbred—used two breeds of an animal to produce a new breed

dressage—a specific kind of horse training; dressage horses perform movements like spins and turns at the command of their riders.

driving horses—horses that pull wagons, carts, carriages, or other vehicles

endurance—the ability to do something for a long time

foundation horse—one of the first horses of a specific breed

harness racing—an event in which a horse pulls a cart and rider

jockeys—people who ride racehorses

Middle Ages—a time period in Europe lasting from the 500s to the 1500s

pole bending—an event in which horses race along a course with six poles arranged in a line; the horses must weave between the poles as fast as they can without knocking them over.

temperament—personality or nature

Triple Crown—the accomplishment of winning the Kentucky Derby, the Preakness Stakes, and the Belmont Stakes in the same year

TO LEARN MORE

At the Library

Farrell, Russell. *Learn to Draw Horses & Ponies*. Irvine, Calif.: Walter Foster Pub., 2011.

Green, Sara. *The Lipizzan Horse*. Minneapolis, Minn.: Bellwether Media, 2012.

Littlefield, Cindy A. *Horse Games & Puzzles*. North Adams, Mass.: Storey Publishing, 2004.

On the Web

Learning more about horses is as easy as 1, 2, 3.

1. Go to www.factsurfer.com.

2. Enter "horses" into the search box.

3. Click the "Surf" button and you will see a list of related Web sites.

With factsurfer.com, finding more information is just a click away.

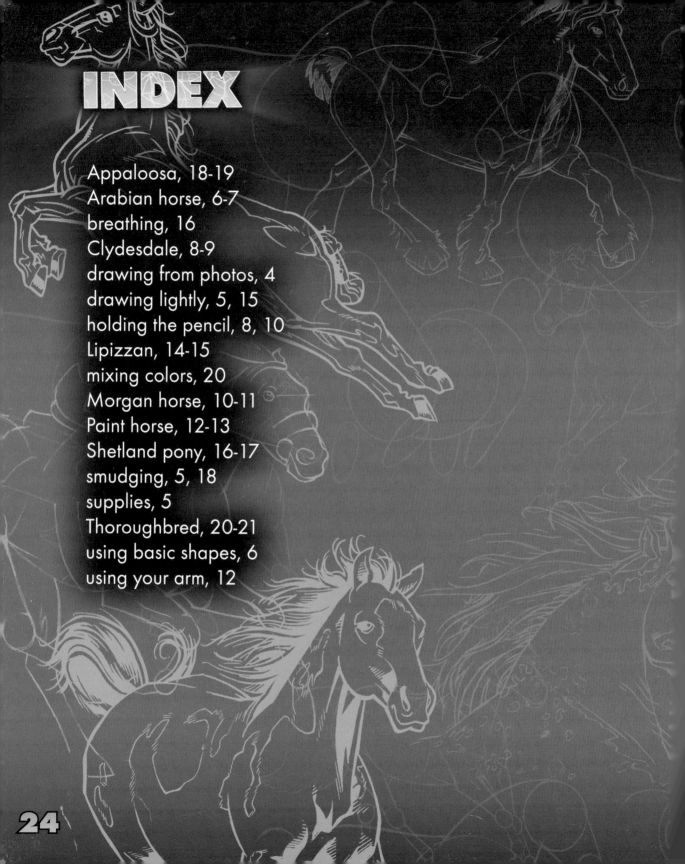

INDEX